Incredible Experiments with
Chemical
Reactions and Mixtures

Text: Paula Navarro & Àngels Jiménez
Illustrations: Bernadette Cuxart

Contents

Objectives of this book

We present you with the third book in the series of four "Magic Science" volumes.

Incredible Experiments with Chemical Reactions and Mixtures aims to enable boys and girls aged from 6 to 12 years old to make their initial journey into the spectacular and fascinating world of chemistry.

With this book, they will be able to go into science even further and become familiar with this important subject firsthand. They will make mixtures and discover components, chemical processes, and more!

They will also learn and understand a large number of phenomena as they experiment with materials that are easy to obtain. They will become familiar with new concepts that are approached in a simple and interesting way, through household experiments.

Incredible Experiments with Chemical Reactions and Mixtures presents 16 stimulating experiments in which the boys and girls become little scientific researchers and get used to working with procedures and operations used in the laboratory. The world of chemistry is accessible in this volume!

You will need:
- Vinegar
- Eggs
- A glass or glass container
- A permanent marker
- A plate
- A flashlight

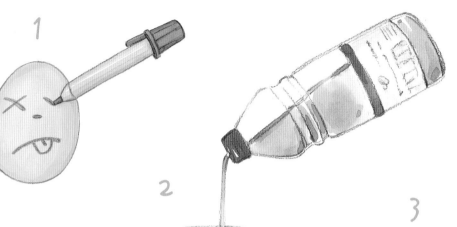

1 Decorate the egg a little to make the experiment more fun! We've drawn a sad face, because he doesn't know what he's in for… poor thing!

2 Then carefully place it at the bottom of the container so that it doesn't break. Oh, and you can place more than one egg if you like! Pour a little vinegar into the container. There should be enough vinegar to cover the egg(s). Bathe it in vinegar!

3 If you look carefully, you will see that bubbles form on the eggshell that rise up to the surface of the vinegar… The reaction is starting! Even though it might smell a bit strong, you should leave the egg in the vinegar for 2 or 3 days, but you must change the vinegar regularly to obtain the desired effect.

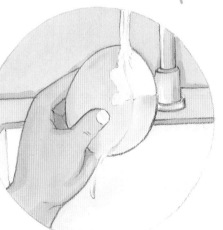

4 After 2 or 3 days, empty the container, holding your nose. Pooh! Be careful not to break the egg. Wash the egg well, because it will be covered in a white layer. Now the egg is larger and softer!

5 Hold the egg carefully in one hand and a flashlight in the other. If you focus the light well, you will see that the yolk can be seen clearly. It's also very pretty... Ooh...

Why does it happen?

The vinegar contains an acid called **acetic acid** that **reacts** with and combines with the eggshell, which is made of **calcium carbonate**. As a result of this reaction a gas is released, and that's why bubbles form around the egg after a few minutes. As the hours pass, the eggshell is completely dissolved and an elastic membrane remains, transforming the fragile egg into a bouncing ball! Also, the membrane is **permeable** and allows water to enter. That's why the egg is larger!

6 Try it out!

Lastly, hold the egg two hands away and you will see that it bounces on the plate. It's like a ball! Hey! But if you throw it too hard or from far away, the egg will break, of course. It's still a real egg, OK?

Colorful milk

You will need:
- Milk
- Water
- Food coloring, inks, or watercolors
- Dishwashing liquid
- A large container
- Cotton swabs
- 2 small containers
- 2 teaspoons

1 Pour a little milk into the large container so that the bottom is covered plus a little more—about three fingers' width high. Ooh! Don't dunk your cookies in it, no matter how tempting it looks!

2 In one of the small containers, place a little water and a little coloring, in a bright color so that it contrasts with the color of the milk. The water must be completely dyed. Do so with two colors.

3 With a teaspoon, take a little dyed water and pour it on the milk... You will see that its color spreads through the milk! Then take the other color and pour a little over the first.

4 Dip the tip of the cotton swab into the dishwashing liquid so that it is well soaked.

5 As if it were a magic wand, touch the tip of the cotton swab with the dishwashing liquid on it into the milk and dye mixture, right in the middle. You will see that the dye opens up, forming an "O." It looks like the color is fleeing from the dishwashing liquid! Maybe it's scared of it!

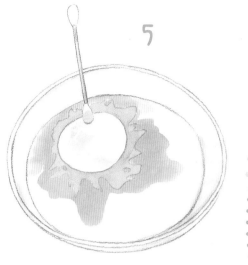

Why does it happen?

The milk contains fats that prevent the dye from **dissolving**, that is, from breaking down. That's why you see it so clearly. It also contains a lot of water and it forms a kind of skin, in the same way that when you dive into the swimming pool it hurts when you hit it. This skin also enables pond skaters and other insects to walk on the water. It is called **surface tension**. You break this skin of water with the dishwashing liquid, and that's why the colors form shapes and mix together.

6 Try it out!

Try wetting the cotton swab with the dishwashing liquid on it at different parts of the colored milk, leaving it in for more or less time… and watch as abstract shapes are formed! You are a modern artist!

Bubble lifter

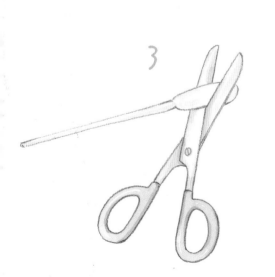

1 Pour a glass of vinegar into the container and then add a couple of teaspoons of bicarbonate of soda.

2 You will see that a foamy reaction soon takes place. You have to cover the container right away, because the vinegar and the bicarbonate of soda are producing carbon dioxide and it must not escape. Leave the mixture to react in the container for about thirty seconds.

You will need:
- A container with a lid
- Vinegar
- Dishwashing liquid
- Bicarbonate of soda
- Scissors
- A teaspoon
- A glass of warm water
- Sugar
- A pipette (from the drug store) or a bubble blower

3 Cut the broad part of the pipette in half so that the pipette is open at both ends and you can blow through them, more or less like a flute, but more basic...

4 Prepare the liquid to make the bubbles. In the glass of warm water, add two fingers' width of dishwashing liquid and also a little sugar, less than half a teaspoon. Don't overdo it!

5 Wet the wide part of the pipette in the mixture of water, dishwashing liquid, and sugar and try blowing bubbles. Try to keep the bubbles from breaking! You have to be patient, blow slowly, and release the bubble.

Why does it happen?

When you mix the vinegar and the bicarbonate of soda, a gas is released, **carbon dioxide** (which is invisible), and creates the foam. This gas is the same as the one you release when you breathe out and is denser than air; it is heavier. That's why when the reaction takes place inside the container, this gas accumulates at the bottom and forms a bed for the bubbles, which, thanks to their shape and lightness, support one another. Given that the carbon dioxide is transparent, they appear to rise up, as if by magic!

6 Try it out!

Now that you know how to make bubbles with the pipette, you can carefully take the lid off the container. Move the pipette toward the middle of the container, hold it above it, and observe the bubbles forming. Wow! The bubbles rise! How is this possible?

Let's play with starch!

1 Place one of the containers on the scale and pour about 3½ ounces of water into it. To measure the amount, first weigh the empty container and then subtract the amount of water you pour in from the total.

You will need:
- A microwave
- Corn starch
- Water
- 3 small or medium containers
- Food coloring or ink
- Scale
- Plastic wrap
- A teaspoon
- Tape
- Scissors

2 Pour the starch into the other container, the same amount as the water, about 3½ ounces. Mix it all together with a teaspoon until you obtain a thin paste.

3 The dough is ready when you obtain the following effect: When you place two fingers in the mixture slowly, you will see that they sink in; but if you hit it hard with your fingers, you will see that they don't sink in, but it appears hard and the fingers bounce off! If necessary, add a little more starch.

4 Continue experimenting with the starch… Now add half a teaspoon of coloring and mix it well. Red will look really cool!

5 Place the colored dough in the microwave at moderate strength for about a minute. Leave it to cool and then make a ball with your hands, removing the parts that are too hard or burnt.

Why does it happen?

To make the ball, you mixed 50% water and starch, that is, you added the same amount of water as starch. The water guzzled so much flour that in the end it could guzzle no more! As a result of this, you obtained a mixture that is neither liquid nor solid, but rather that has **viscosity**, that is the ease of movement, to change as you apply more or less force to it. When this happens, you are said to have a **Newtonian fluid**. Did you know that ketchup is also one? But it works the other way!

6 Try it out!

Cut a piece of plastic wrap and wrap the ball in it. Wrap it around so that it is tense and fasten it around the ball with tape. If the plastic wrap is too long, cut it. Now your ball is ready to bounce!

1 + 1 is not 2!

1 With a ruler, measure the height of the glass into which you pour the water. We have measured 6 cm from the bottom and marked it with a pen.

2 Do the same with the other glass, into which you pour the alcohol. When the lines are marked on both glasses, write the number 1 on them.

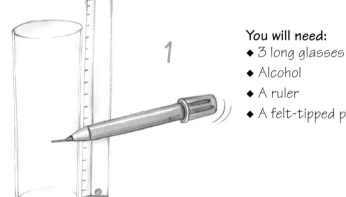

1

You will need:
- 3 long glasses
- Alcohol
- A ruler
- A felt-tipped pen

2

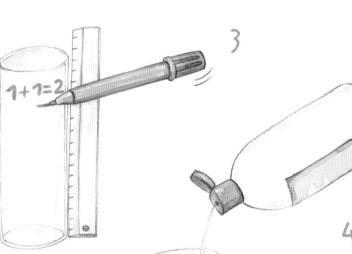

3

4

3 On the third glass, measure 12 cm from the bottom of the glass and write on the mark: 1 + 1 = 2. You do so because you measured 6 cm in the two previous glasses and because the sum of 6 + 6 is 12… just as the sum of 1 + 1 = 2.

4 Pour some alcohol into one of the glasses, up to the mark you have made (which was 6 cm). It's best to crouch down a little to see the line at eye level.

5 Pour a little warm water into the other marked glass. It doesn't need to be boiling! The warm water from the tap will do!

5

1

Why does it happen?

Two liquids that can be mixed together are called **miscible**! When the water from one of the glasses is added with the alcohol in the other glass, the two liquids mix and the volume that each of them had separately is reduced when they come into contact. If you looked at it through a microscope, you would see that the water particles separate and embrace those of the alcohol so that they occupy less space. This difference means that 1 + 1 is not 2!

6 Try it out!

Pour the liquids from each glass, the glass of water and the glass of alcohol, into the glass you have marked with the sum of the two, the one with 1 + 1 = 2. The accumulation of these two liquids should add up and hence reach the line you've marked on the glass, but... but... It's a very simple sum! Well, in this case, you cannot say that 1 plus 1 is 2! Ah... Would it have something to do with the bubbles you see in the mixture of the two liquids? Or in the warm water?... Or what?

6

A beret for a coin

1 Fill the dropper with water and test it to master how to handle it... If you place it in the container and squeeze the rubber part, the liquid rises; if you stop pressing it, the liquid stays in the same place. Then if your remove the dropper from the container and squeeze the rubber part again, the liquid falls in drops. Yes, you can do it!

You will need:
- A jug full of water
- Dishwashing liquid
- A dropper
- A penny
- A paper clip

2 Place the coin flat, and with the dropper place drops of water on it. See how many drops of water fit on the surface. We managed to place 13 drops before the water spilled over!

3 Fill the surface of the coin with water again, slowly. But this time do so and stop just before the meniscus (the surface curve) of the water breaks. So there will be 11 or 12 drops. Don't lose count!

4 Open the paper clip so that there is a point upward, like a needle but without a sharp point.

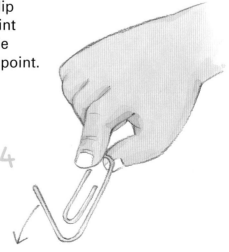

5 Place the tip of the clip on the center of the beret you've made with the water on the coin... and you will see that, despite the fact that the clip is touching the water, it doesn't spill over. Oooh! How is this possible?

6 Try it out!
Wet the paper clip in the dishwashing liquid and repeat the process: Place it in the beret on the coin. Now, on the contrary, the water beret breaks quickly! It doesn't last at all!

Why does it happen?

As you add the drops of water on the coin, they join together, covered in a "skin" of water. The **surface tension** of the water enables the mushroom-shaped beret to form, and the same thing enables a paper clip to float in a glass full of water. But everything has its limit, of course. If you add too many drops, the skin cannot cover them and it breaks! The same thing happens when you touch it with the dishwashing liquid, which causes the skin to break and the coin to be left with its head uncovered!

You go up and I go down

You will need:
- ◆ A large transparent container
- • Two small containers with lids
- • A glass
- • Some marbles
- • A teaspoon
- • Blue and red food coloring

1 Fill the large clear container with water, but NOT completely! Leave about 3 fingers' width without water.

2 Now fill a glass with marbles or similar objects that weigh a bit. Place the glass inside the container of water and they will serve as a "pedestal" to support another container on top.

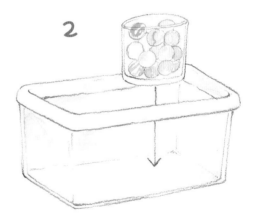

3 In one of the small containers, prepare a mixture of hot water and half a teaspoon of red colorant. Place a few marbles inside the container and close it.

4 Then mix cold water with the blue colorant. It's important to maintain the temperature difference between the water in the two containers and to have two contrasting colors. Also place a few marbles inside and close it.

5 Place the closed containers inside the large container in the following way: the one with the red colorant at the bottom and the one with the blue colorant supported on the glass of marbles. They should both be horizontal and facing one another, like in the picture. Now you understand why you put the marbles in the containers, don't you? To stop them from floating! Then finish filling the large container with water at room temperature.

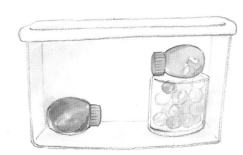

5

Why does it happen?

You have hot red water and cold blue water in a container filled with water at room temperature. **The hot water is less dense than the room temperature water and thus weighs less and tends to rise, whereas the cold water is denser, weighs more, and sinks.** The same thing happens in the atmosphere with air masses and at the bottom of the ocean! Thanks to this, there are clouds and ocean currents, and that's why we place air conditioners high up on the wall!

6 Try it out!
Concentrate and quickly unscrew the lids of both containers at the same time... 1, 2, 3... NOW! Remove the lids and observe how the colored liquids flow freely. Where does the blue liquid go? And the red?

6

Bigheaded bottle

1 Choose a balloon in a color you like and draw a funny face on it. We've drawn a smiley face, as he will have a lot of fun in this experiment!

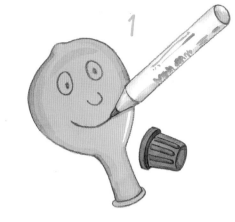

You will need:
- ◆ A half-liter bottle of soda
- • A small container
- • A permanent marker
- • Scissors
- • A balloon

2 Open the soda very carefully, without losing the gas! Don't shake it before you open it or open it upside down… as all of the gas and bubbles will come out and you'll get wet!

3 Remove the ring around the bottle opening, as you won't need it for the experiment. You can remove it with your fingers or with the help of the scissors. Snip!

4 Remove a little soda from the bottle, pouring it into the small container: about 4 fingers' width. Don't worry, it doesn't need to be exact…

Why does it happen?

Soda is a drink that contains carbonated water. And what's that? Well, it's water that contains a gas, carbon dioxide, dissolved in it; that is, there is a lot of carbon dioxide mixed with the water. When you shake the bottle with the balloon in place, the balloon inflates even more. It didn't just get fat suddenly! This happens because **the gas that is dissolved in the water has separated and has been released!** The gas tries to leave the bottle and the only way out is into the balloon. And because the balloon is elastic, it inflates on its own!

5 Place the balloon opening over the neck of the bottle so that it is well secured and the balloon doesn't shoot off.

6 Try it out!
Hold the neck of the bottle with the balloon with one hand, just in case… and shake the bottle strongly so that the gas enters the balloon. If you leave the bottle on the table, you will see the balloon blow up, as if by magic! You have a bigheaded balloon!

Lonely oil

1 Place some oil in the small container. Just a little… about two or three fingers' width, as this oil might be useful for frying an egg!

2 Now take the large glass and mark a line on it with the pen, about halfway, so you don't need a ruler… Do so by sight. This glass will serve to measure the volume and to know where to separate the two liquids you're going to pour in.

3 Pour some water in, up to the line, trying to be accurate and not to spill the water!

4 Then you have to pour the alcohol on top of the water. It's very important that the alcohol is cold for the experiment to work, and so you should place it in the fridge for a while until it feels quite cool when you touch it.

5

Why does it happen?

The cold alcohol is not as miscible in water; it is harder for it to mix. That's why when you pour in the water and then the cold alcohol, two different layers form. When you introduce the oil with the syringe, this is more dense than the alcohol and less dense than the water, so it is trapped between the two layers, completely alone.
Given that **the alcohol and the water compress the oil in the same way on both sides**, you obtain a lovely circle of oil!

5 When the alcohol is cold, pour it into the glass with the water, pouring about the same amount of alcohol as water. They look like twin brothers… It's difficult to distinguish them without touching the glass, isn't it?

6 Try it out!

This step is very delicate! You have to submerge the syringe in the oil and suck it up into the plunger so that it fills with oil and then carefully introduce the syringe into the middle of the glass, exactly between the water and the alcohol. Gradually, press down the plunger leaving one or two bubbles of oil in the middle. Wow! What has happened? The oil has been left completely alone in between the other two liquids!

6

Let's purify the water!

You will need:
- A jug of water
- Large plastic glasses
- A funnel
- A piece of plastic tube
- Tape
- Scissors
- A felt-tipped pen
- A sheet of plastic
- A piece of cotton fabric
- Elastic bands
- A sieve
- Small clean stones
- Samples of soil, large stones, and leaves

1 The first thing you have to do to purify the water is... to dirty it! So, add some soil, stones, and leaves to the clean water.

2 Make the first filter, which will serve to clean the water. Draw a circle on the sheet of plastic and cut it out. Place the plastic with holes made in it over an empty glass and pour the dirty water through it: You will see that the leaves and largest stones remain on the filter.

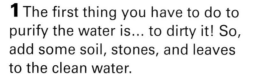

3 Make the second water filter, this time with the strainer. Pour the water through the strainer and now the smaller residues are left on it.

4 The next filter is harder to make. Insert the piece of plastic tube into the funnel and secure it with tape. Then, use the scissors to make some little holes along the tube and block the end with tape.

22

5 Place the funnel with the tube in a large glass and beside it place the small stones. It's important that they are very clean! Add stones until all the little holes in the tube are covered. Pour the water you have just filtered into the funnel... and you will see that the water that rises is cleaner!

Why does it happen?

In water purifying plants, the water you drink has gone through processes very similar to what you have just done! In the first place, the largest filter removes the largest dirtiness and the smallest removes the medium-sized impurities. With the tube and small stones, you made a device that cleans the water by **filtration** (the water passes between the stones and the impurities are trapped between them) and by **settling** (the water remains on top and can be separated from the rest). And lastly, the fabric removes the smallest impurities! But don't drink the water, because further steps still would be needed to make it drinkable!

6 Try it out!

The last filter is finer and you make it with the fabric. Place the folded fabric over a clean glass and secure it around the top with several elastic bands. Shape it like a funnel with your fingers and then pour in the filtered water. What's the result? The water is much cleaner than before... Yes, yes! It's almost transparent! Good!

23

Homemade ice cream...Mmm!

1 First, place all the ingredients in the small ziplock bag together to obtain the ice cream. We'll make chocolate ice cream! So, first add the chocolate milkshake (previously shaken). Then add the liquid cream and 3 teaspoons of sugar.

You will need:
- Chocolate milkshake
- Liquid cream
- Ice cubes
- Sugar
- Salt
- Scissors
- A small glass container
- Two ziplock bags (one larger than the other)
- A teaspoon

2 Close the ziplock bag well and shake the three ingredients vigorously! Up, down, up, down... You exercise your arms at the same time!

3 Insert the closed bag you've just shaken into the large ziplock bag. Then add the ice cubes so that the small bag is surrounded by them. You need quite a lot of ice cubes!

4 Add 3 teaspoons of salt to the ice cubes. Don't get mixed up with the sugar jar, otherwise the ice cream won't work.

Why **does it happen?**

The ice cools the ingredients of the ice cream, but to freeze them you need it to be even colder! Brrr! That's why you add the salt, to lower the **freezing point** of the water below 32°F and make it even colder for your ice cream! That's why salt is used in ice cream trucks. The freezing point is lowered and the ice melts first!

5 Close the large plastic bag well and put on some gloves, now that you must hold the bag for a while. Shake the bag for at least 10 minutes.

6 Try it out!
Then you can pour the contents of the small bag into a bowl. The 3 ingredients have been converted into an ice cream or mousse... Ready to eat! Mmm!

An explosive orange!

1 Fill your lungs with air and blow up the balloon. Make it as large as you can!

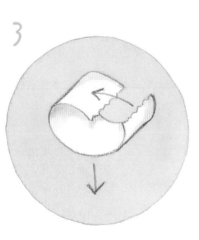

2 Draw a face on it with the pen or draw whatever you like. We've drawn a sad face, because this balloon isn't going to like what's in store for him...

3 Cut out a piece of tape and make a circle from it like an "O," being careful to avoid sticking your fingers to it. Then stick it on the table or a flat surface.

4 Stick the back of the balloon (without the face) onto the tape you've just stuck on the table. Then the balloon will stay in place!

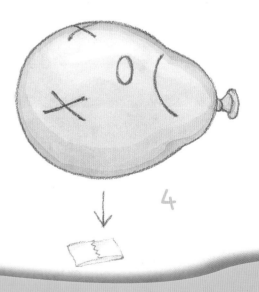

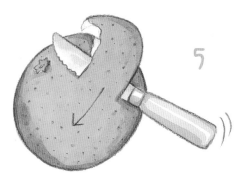

5 With a peeler or a knife and with the help of an adult, cut off some of the orange peel. A piece the size of a palm is large enough. Then you'll be able to eat the orange! It will be very good!

6 Try it out!
Hold the orange peel in both hands, stand about two hands distance from the balloon, and squeeze the peel very strongly— as if you were making juice! BOOM! Suddenly, the balloon bursts! That's why he had such a sad face—what an orange!

Why *does* it happen?
Orange peel contains an acid called limonene. And it's not just found in oranges! It's also found in lemons, limes, mandarins, and grapefruits… It's an acid so strong that it acts as a **solvent** on the latex of the balloon, that is, it breaks it down! Latex is a material that is found in nature and is made from tree resin. It is very flexible, and that's why the balloon has to be blown up very large and tense, because then it is easier for the limonene to dissolve it and make it burst!

In search of the secret message...

You will need:
- Starch or flour
- A jug of water
- Iodine
- A lemon
- A glass
- Cotton swabs
- Paper towel
- Aluminum foil

1 Pour two fingers' width of water into the glass and add 2 heaped teaspoons of starch.

1

2 Then stir the mixture of water and starch so that you are not left with any lumps!

2

3 Wet the tip of a cotton swab in the glass where you have the mixture. Immediately write a sentence on the paper towel, as if the cotton swab were a pencil! It will be a secret message, because the text is not visible at the moment! Don't tell anybody!

3

4 When you want to reveal the message, slowly pour a little iodine (the same as that used for wounds) on the paper towel. It might be easier with a clean unused cotton swab! Apply the iodine to one end of the paper and wet the whole area with the hidden sentence...

4

5

5 When the area is covered in iodine, you will see that the secret message is no longer a secret! It has become visible and it's dark brown in color! Now cut the lemon in half: We're going to explain a trick to you…

6 Try it out!
How could you make the message invisible again without leaving any trace of it? Well, rub the whole sentence with the half lemon (it would be better to place aluminum foil underneath to avoid dirtying the table). Gradually, the sentence disappears! It's worthy of the best spy in the world!

Why does it happen?

When the iodine mixes with the starch in the message, a dark brown-colored substance is obtained. The secret letters are then dyed with color and you can read the hidden message, as if you were detectives and you were trying to solve a case! The lemon contains vitamin C and it reacts with the iodine. But this time, the substance obtained is transparent and that's why the message disappears again. Now you know that if you stain yourself with iodine, you can clean it with lemon juice!

6

Mysterious column

You will need:

- Alcohol
- Honey
- Dishwashing liquid
- Oil
- Water
- Colorant
- A teaspoon
- A normal glass
- A tall glass
- Different kinds of balls

1 The first thing you pour into the tall glass is two fingers' width of honey... Yum, how sweet!

2 Then add some dishwashing liquid, also a couple of fingers' width. You'll see that the dishwashing liquid stays on top of the honey, without mixing with it! And the color contrast is fun!

3 The third liquid is the water, but with red coloring! Then you'll be able to distinguish the colors well. Add a little coloring and two fingers' width of water. Then pour it on top of your strange column.

4 Now pour in the fourth liquid. It's the oil's turn! Pour it carefully, down the side of the glass, and you'll see that everything stays without mixing!

Why does it happen?

By combining liquids of different **densities** that are also **immiscible**—that is, they do not mix together—you obtain a very pretty column of liquids that are positioned layer by layer in order of density. The lightest, the less dense goes at the top; lower down, the layer is denser and weighs more. When you drop objects into the column (rubber balls, plastic foam, drawing pins, and marbles), the following occurs: According to their density and their shape, they stay in one place or another!

5 And finally, the last liquid: the alcohol! Leave it transparent, because the other liquids are colored. You'll see that despite the fact that you leave it for a while, the 5 liquids remain intact, each occupying its space without bothering the others.

6 Try it out!

Drop the different balls you have prepared: more and less heavy, large and small, etc. You can also drop other things to see in which liquid they are trapped! Or guess with friends: Will it stay in the honey? In the oil? In the water? This column is a mystery…

The apple is withered... What's wrong with it?

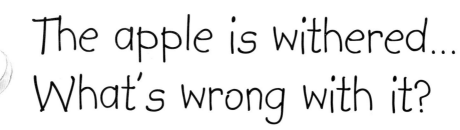

1 Cut the apple in half. To do so, it's best for an adult to help you so you don't cut your fingers! There! You should have two more or less equal pieces.

You will need:
- A jug of water
- A glass
- A lemon
- An apple
- A knife

2 Also cut the lemon in half and squeeze one half into a glass. Don't drink the juice, as you need it for the experiment—and also it tastes *very* bitter!

3 Add water to the lemon juice, filling the glass almost completely. Now the lemon juice is watered down and clearer, but it will be perfect for the experiment.

4 Place one half of the apple in the glass with the lemon and water. Do so carefully so that it doesn't splash!

Why does it happen?

When a substance is mixed with another to form something different, a **chemical reaction** takes place, and if oxygen enters into play, this process is called **oxidation**. The apple did not get sick and it didn't have a bellyache, no! It has reacted with the oxygen in the air; **it has oxidized**. Lemon contains citric acid, which loves playing with oxygen. When you wet the apple in the lemonade, this acid does what it likes the best and it combines with the oxygen, preventing this from ruining the apple.

5 Now we will wait a while until the piece of apple outside the liquid starts to turn brown.

5

6

6 Try it out!

When you see that the piece of apple outside the glass has a slightly dark tone, it's time to remove the other piece of apple from the glass, wait a while, and then compare the two pieces. What do you see? The half that was soaked is the same as before! This lemon bath seems to have done it some good!

33

A telltale in the Kitchen

You will need:

- Boiled purple cabbage water
- Lemonade
- Water
- Bicarbonate of soda
- A teaspoon
- 3 small glasses

1 Pour a little lemonade into one of the small glasses you have prepared: Half a glass will do; you don't need the rest of the lemonade. You can share it with your friends. Great!

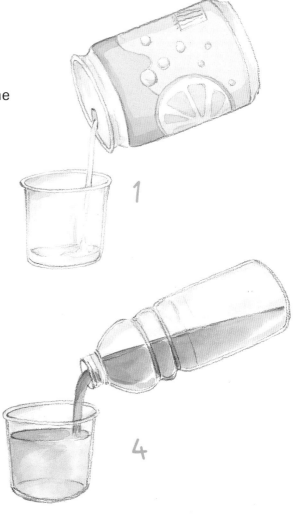

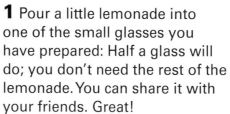

2 In the other glass, add a little bicarbonate of soda to the water and mix them with the teaspoon. The taste is not as good as the last one, so we don't advise tasting it. Yuck!

3 Pour the boiled purple cabbage water into the third glass… When you open it, you'll notice that it has quite a disgusting smell. So it's not good to drink either.

4 The moment for mixing has arrived! Take the boiled purple cabbage water and pour a little into the glass containing the water and bicarbonate of soda. What happens?

5 Do the same thing, but with the lemonade: Pour in a little boiled purple cabbage water… And now? What color does it turn?

Why **does** it happen?

In nature, things are divided into **acids** and **bases**. Lemon juice, Coca-cola, vinegar, and hydrochloric acid… are acids: They have a sour taste and break down metals. Bleach, ammonia, bicarbonate of soda, and caustic soda… are bases. They have a bitter taste and break down fats, which is why many of them are cleaning products. To find out whether you have an acid or a base, you can't taste it, because it would be dangerous! Some liquids, like boiled purple cabbage water, tell us that: If it changes red, it's an acid; if it changes blue, it's a base!

6 Try it out!

If you place the three glasses side by side, you will see three very pretty colors: pink, green, and lilac! But you didn't have these colors at the start! Which is the pink liquid? In any case, the result is very PRETTY!

Try it at home with other things: Pour the boiled purple cabbage water onto an egg, an orange, some toothpaste mixed with water… See what effects you obtain!

Incredible Experiments with
Chemical
Reactions and Mixtures

First edition for the United States and Canada published in 2014 by Barron's Educational Series, Inc.

Copyright © Gemser Publications, S.L. 2014
C/ Castell, 38; Teià (08329) Barcelona, Spain (World Rights)
Tel: 93 540 13 53
E-mail: info@mercedesros.com
Website: mercedesros.com

Text: Paula Navarro & Àngels Jiménez

Illustrations: Bernadette Cuxart

Design and layout: Estudi Guasch, S.L.

All inquiries should be addressed to:
Barron's Educational Series, Inc.
250 Wireless Boulevard
Hauppauge, New York 11788
www.barronseduc.com

ISBN: 978-1-4380-0427-3

Library of Congress Control
    Number: 2013943485

Date of Manufacture: May 2014
Place of Manufacture: L. REX PRINTING
    COMPANY LIMITED, Dongguan City,
    Guangdong, China

Printed in China
9 8 7 6 5 4 3 2 1